Contemporary Quilts

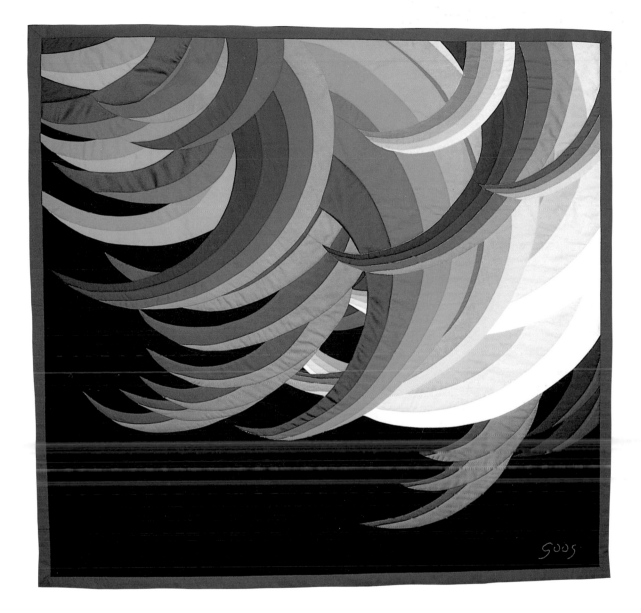

Dedication

To my husband Ian, without whom there would have been no quilt shows and no book.

Acknowledgements

The author would like to thank the sponsors of the Contemporary International Quilt Collection, Pfaff Sewing Machines (U.K.) and Yorkshire Television, for their invaluable support.

The Quilters' Guild

For details of groups in the United Kingdom, contact the Publishers for the Guild's current address.

Opposite: Detail of Girls of Glory *by Ulva Ugerup.*

CONTEMPORARY QUILTS

A stunning collection of quilts from international designers

Compiled by
BARBARA HALLAS

SEARCH PRESS

First published in Great Britain 1994

Search Press Limited
Wellwood, North Farm Road,
Tunbridge Wells, Kent TN2 3DR

Photographs by Search Press Studios with the exception of the
picture on page 9, which was taken by Deirdre Amsden
(before it was quilted).

ISBN 0 85532 774 X

Colour Separated by P&W Graphics Pte Ltd., Singapore
Printed in Spain by Elkar S. Coop, 48013, Bilbao

Contents

Introduction

After organising a large exhibition, by late 1991 I felt that there was a need for a small exhibition of selected quilts rather like those found in Europe. This would 'fill the gap' between the biennial exhibitions organised by the Quilters' Guild and the Shipley Art Gallery, Gateshead, in the north of England. There was a response from twelve countries and finally fifty quilts were selected by Deirdre Amsden, from London, and Lois Auty, from Yorkshire. The work chosen was contemporary and in many cases offered new ideas to quilters.

The International Quilt Collection exhibition was held in 1993 in the Long Room, New College, Oxford, and at Nostell Priory. Approximately half the quilts selected to appear in the exhibition are shown in this book.

There are many excellent publications, including magazines, on how to design and make a particular quilt. This book is a small 'gallery' of modern textile hangings that will help you decide what sort of quilt you want to try next. There is such a variety here that there must be two or three outstanding ones to prompt you to say, 'I'd really like to make one like that.' Even those who claim that they were no good at needlework at school may be stimulated to start sewing a lasting memory of a quilting class, a journey to a place associated with happy memories, or perhaps an intricately curved maze or waterfall.

Paint, dye, or stencil if you want to minimise the piecing, and then draw with your machine-needle or calmly hand quilt. Create something unique and hang it on the wall. Every one of the quilters in this book had to start somewhere! Now make your own start, and I wish you much joy with it.

Barbara Hallas

Colourwash Cuboids and Pink Triangles

DEIRDRE AMSDEN
London, England

Deirdre Amsden was the first president of the Quilters' Guild in Britain and then the first editor of its magazine. She trained at the Cambridge School of Art, then taught herself to quilt; she transferred from illustration to quilt-making in 1976. Her work appears in innumerable books and catalogues in Britain, Europe and the United States; her quilts have been seen in a 'suitcase exhibition' in New Zealand; and she finds time to teach and lecture as well. She remains one of the half-dozen best-known and readily recognised quilters who put patchwork and quilting 'on the map' in Britain about fifteen years ago and who have consistently remained at the top ever since.

Deirdre started quilting using traditional-style designs. Next she developed her variations, and then she went on to original work. She says, 'From the start I was interested in one-patch designs which are typical of English scrap quilts.' Out of this, her delightful *Colourwash* series has developed. The hallmark of her work is the blending rather than the contrasting of hundreds of cotton prints, and the infinitely subtle three-dimensional effects this produces. Most quilters here and abroad covet these beautiful quilts!

In this example of her work, the cuboid shapes form the background for the pink triangles. (There are 420 of the latter!). Here there is one pattern over another. Looking at the quilt, you feel that you could almost climb on to it or into it; or, if you look at it from the side, you could see it as a series of awnings projecting from sunlit buildings. There is really no need for verbal explanations, though; just *looking* gives such pleasure.

Quilting, with all the associated activities it entails, is for Deirdre a full-time job, and her studio is the mezzanine floor of her flat.

Original size: 172 x 147cm (69 x 59in).

Out Here on the Edge of Space with Nancy

JEAN CORBRIDGE

Leeds, England

This quilt is made of cottons and chintzes, hand-pieced over paper templates (the so-called English method) and then hand quilted. The initial idea was taken from a book of Islamic designs; then there were additions and alterations, and many shapes were divided into smaller pieces.

Jean wanted to have stars in each of the wall-hangings she made for her three daughters: her 'stars'. This one, for Nancy, has lilac and purple; Hester's has maroons and pinks, and Pamela's many different blues.

Plastic templates were made for each shape, and in addition two paper ones were cut, one for the finished shape and one, plus seam allowance, for the fabric. The seven big star wheels were constructed first with the addition of small metal plates covered with purple fabric for their centres. Between and overlapping these are smaller stars within a light-coloured hexagon. Together with the three diamond shapes on the circumference of the large wheels they form alternate four- and six-pointed stars.

Jean copes with the increasing complexity of the pattern with ease as she further constructs odd shapes inside the straight border. The pattern originally stopped here but it was enlarged with a more intricate second border which echoes the boxes round the wheels but with a different perspective. Pairs of these alternate with a delicate pin-wheel to complete the outer border.

Jean admires both traditional and contemporary quilts and feels that quilters should sew whatever makes them happy, although she has some reservations about merely copying from books.

As a child Jean was taught a variety of needlework skills by a neighbour. She herself now teaches several adult classes from September to May, including lacemaking and tatting, but she loves the colour possibilities that patchwork and quilting offer. Jean firmly believes that all these activities are therapeutic because they demand 100-per-cent concentration.

Jean is very organised. Her day starts with all household chores being completed, a plan by no means common to all patchworkers! She sews daily in what used to be a daughter's bedroom, leaving about four evenings and the weekend for her family. She has won several awards for her original quilts and miniatures in England and is currently chairwoman of the Night Owl Quilters in Leeds.

What sort of a teacher does she admire? Without hesitation Jean replied, 'One who doesn't hold back.' Pressed as to her views on lectures to quilters, she thought that unless lecturers were offering something new, what was the point?

Jean enjoys not only the designing and sewing, but also the whole camaraderie of quilting: the group meetings, the exhibitions and the ever-increasing network of friends.

Detail of Out Here on the Edge of Space with Nancy.

Original size: (hexagonal) – 195cm (6 ft 6in) in diameter.

Celebrations and Jubilations

EILEEN COSTELLOE

Limerick, Ireland

As this quilt was designed for the tenth anniversary of the Irish Patchwork Society in 1991, it took its name from the theme at the exhibition. Eileen says that she wanted her quilt to be a giant birthday card that would capture the moment when a gift box is opened: the jack-in-a-box jumps on to his swing as fireworks explode and presents shoot in all directions.

This was a favourite with child viewers, as they immediately sensed the excitement of the occasion. The ebullience is infectious, bringing a smile to the lips of most of those who pass by the quilt. Certainly no inhibitions about 'received' techniques and precision piecing seem to interrupt the creative spontaneity of this joyous quilt.

Yet the variety within the surface texture is achieved with great care. Over 190 different fabrics, colours and textures were incorporated. Silks were dyed and fixed with the simple application of a hot iron, and the background is a 'crazy' patchwork of innumerable different black fabrics. Elsewhere, strip piecing was used, then slashed, stitched in a different direction and slashed again until the desired effect was achieved.

The quilt is busy with small areas of interest: a box made of satin quadrilaterals of rainbow colours sewn together with a machined herringbone stitch. Waiting to be claimed are more presents and a candy walking-stick, while ribbons and rouleaux spin out like Catherine wheels. Metallic threads zigzag outwards – unmistakably sparklers. A cracker and a striped bandbox with a neat scalloped edge tempt one to touch.

If this quilt hangs freely there are further delights on the reverse side. Appliquéd here are shiny, coloured satin envelopes containing stitched and beribboned 'secret' correspondence. If this piece were on a child's bed, what better hiding-place for small treasures?

Detail of Celebrations and Jubilations.

Original size: 132 x 167cm (53 x 67in).

Snail's Trail in my Garden

SHARON DOYLE

California, U.S.A.

On this quilt, the pieced Snail's Trail (or 'Monkey Wrench') blocks are constructed in a unique way. At the end of the exhibition so many quilters were clamouring to know how it was done that a workshop was arranged within a few days. Fortunately Sharon, as an exhibitor, was already in Yorkshire to see the 1993 collection of Contemporary International Quilts.

Sharon's inspiration was her own garden in the early morning, when the much-hated snails have left their wonderfully iridescent trails in the sunlight. The quilt was for a Santa Barbara challenge: 'Each participant was given three "ugly" fabrics which had to compose at least fifty per cent of the quilt-top. Three additional fabrics were allowed, one being a "geometric" print. The surface could be altered, dyed, painted, embellished, etc., as long as it was still recognisable.'

The 'ugly' prints were: (1) a small blue/gold floral; (2) a brown and pink pedestal with birds; and (3) a camel/blue/rust fruit-and-flower print.

One problem was that Sharon's own fabrics were soon used up, but she managed to solve this by taking scraps of the given fabric to make the inner border. This she transformed by using a rubber stamp with a snail picture, to which she added iridescent trails. The 'ugly' prints make a pleasing cultivation and were much admired by visitors. The 7.5cm (3in) Snail Trail rubber stamps were used on a plain muslin (known as calico in the U.K.). This 7.5cm (3in) square was divided into smaller squares and triangles and each was numbered. Selected pieces of fabric were placed on the unprinted side and machined or hand-sewn along the appropriate printed line, one at a time and in order, until the design was assembled. Sharon has a small business that produces these stamps.

Detail of Snail's Trail in my Garden.

Original size: 90 x 90cm (36 x 36in).

Handling the pieces is not difficult as they are first cut to a manageable size and further trimmed when sewn: an easy way to make miniatures.

Asked about the direction in which contemporary quilting might move, she queried the wide use of the word 'quilt', and although she was happy to accept new ideas, Sharon did not care for quilts made using cork, feathers and other non-quilted embellishments. Her own work is likely to explore further the use of printing and painting, thus creating her own textiles.

Sharon teaches across the U.S.A. and in the U.K. She has sewn her own clothes since she was eleven years old; she has designed clothes for a manufacturer; and then she went on to be an architectural/graphic designer. She seems to have boundless energy and spends a fair amount of time travelling. Her dream, however, is to have a studio away from home, free from the telephone and other disruptions, where she could work for six to eight hours a day on developing her many ideas into finished projects.

La Hola

DOMINIQUE FIEVET-MAHOUX
Tarn, France

I think this small quilt illustrates the cheerful greeting 'Hello' superbly. The theme, says Dominique, is 'Les jeux Olympiques': the Olympic Games.

This square seems to be made up of two triangles. The lower one, at first glance, resembles crazy patchwork. Closer observation reveals heads, shoulders, arms and the backs of a crowd of people as they look up at balloons in the other triangle of the night sky above. The black background does in fact have printed coloured circles on it, and Dominique has quilted round these and also chain-stitched zigzag 'streamers' down to the upstretched arms. The figures themselves are appliquéd in carefully grouped coloured cottons and are outlined in black thread quilting in 'the ditch'.

This happy little wall-hanging demonstrates an imaginative way of using printed fabric.

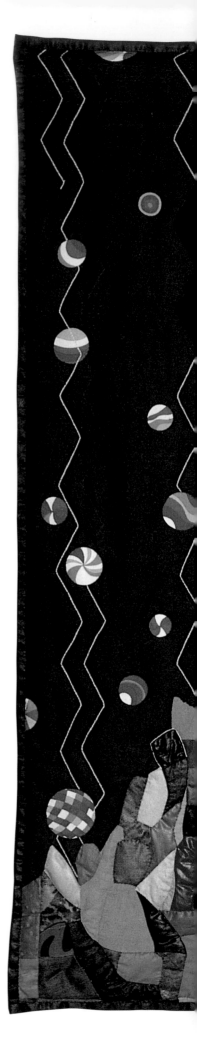

Original size: 85 x 85cm (34 x 34in).

16

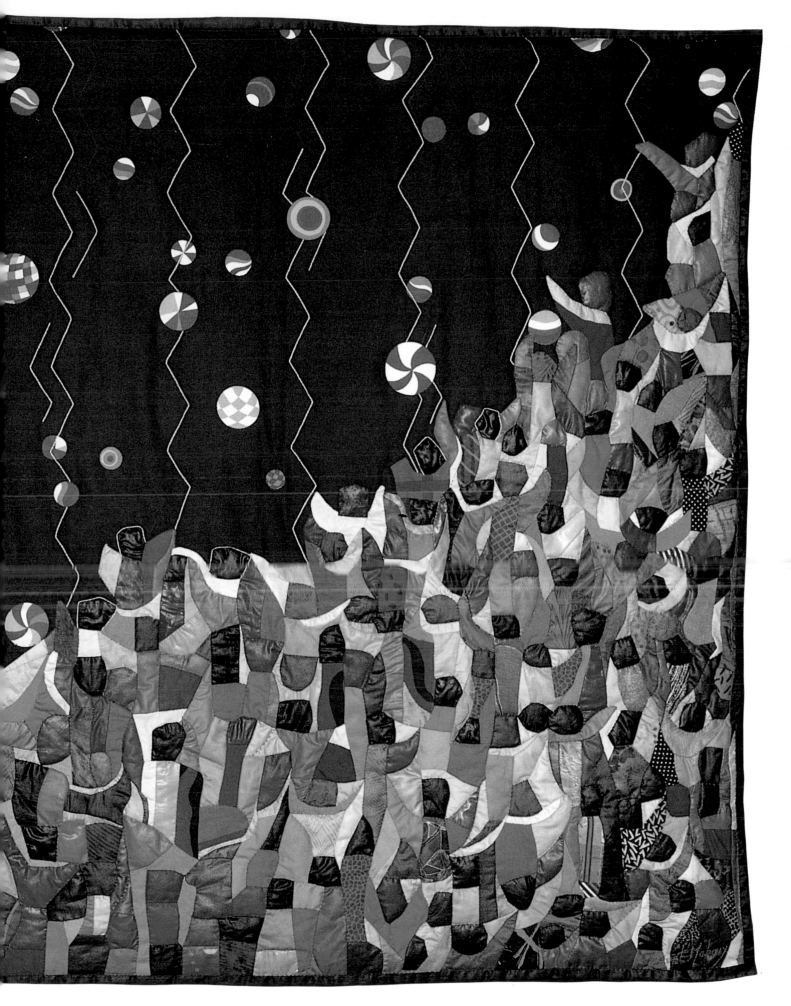

Subway

DOMINIQUE FIEVET-MAHOUX
Tarn, France

Dominique's printed fabric in maroon, with what appear to be black networks, is a textile map of an imaginary underground railway system. There are no names or symbols, so travelling on it might be a bizarre Kafkaesque experience. Alternatively, it could be fun! Or perhaps it is a game where place names have to be provided before the quickest route to X has to be negotiated – who knows?

At any rate, it sets up a situation that provokes questions and the observer feels compelled to solve the 'mystery'. Certainly it is exciting to touch the three-dimensional surface of this quilt.

The padded tubes, approximately 2.5cm (1in) in diameter, can be constructed by the trapunto method. This consists of padding a stitched outlined space between two fabrics. More restrictive or sophisticated definitions are available, but an embossed design is the end product. The stuffing is usually eased in from the back of the work, with the aperture closed afterwards.

The resurgence of trapunto quilting in the 1990s is likely to produce innovative techniques, so that the 'best' way is that which achieves the desired result most efficiently.

A close look at the subway reveals twelve circles that suggest major stations, and two different lines, one moving across the quilt independent of the red tubes and a finer one entwined around these tubes – perhaps an escape route? Everything is kept within bounds by a densely quilted border.

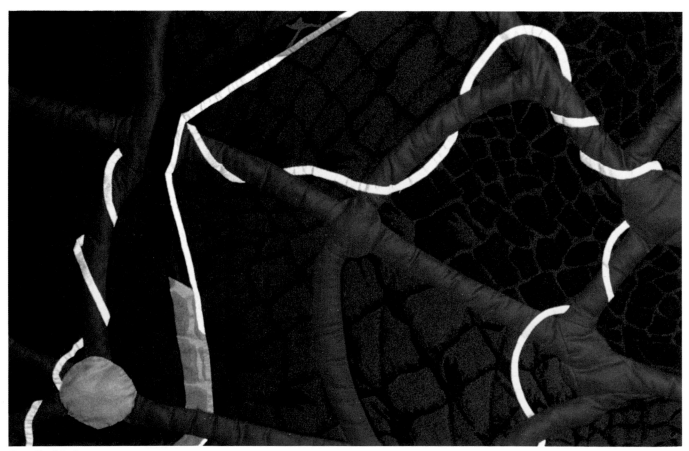

Detail of Subway.

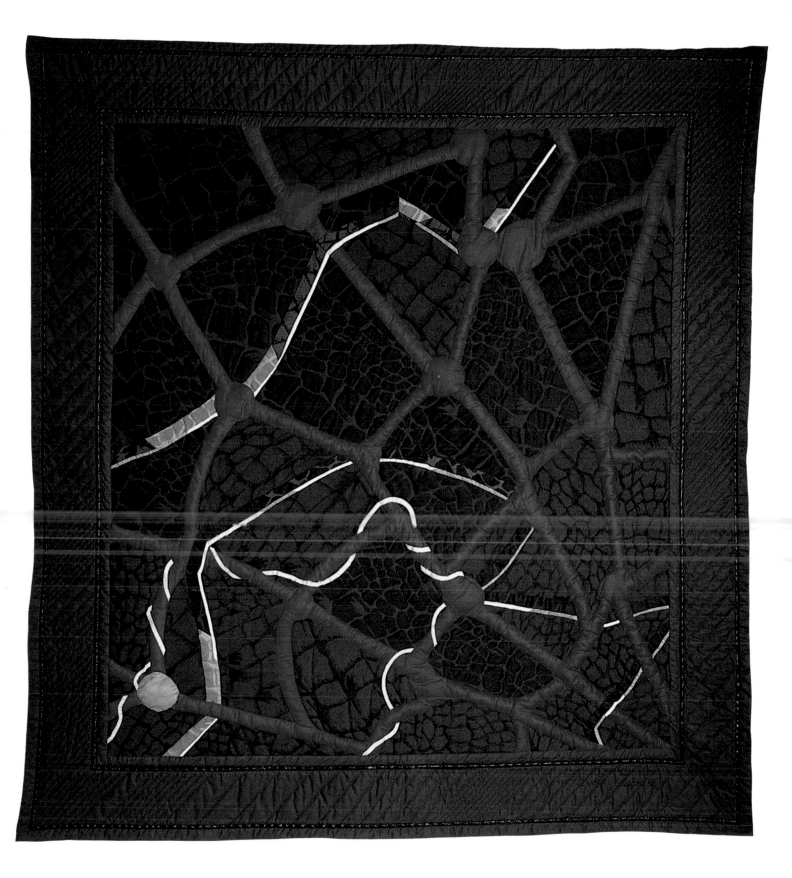

Original size: 152 x 127cm (61 x 51in).

The City

MARY FOGG
Surrey, England

This is a quilt that makes you smile: it is a clever, witty interpretation of contemporary office blocks and the Savile-Row-clad gentlemen who make a living therein.

Mary was given these high-quality suitings, which fitted her current series, 'exploring the expressive possibilities of men's clothing materials'. There is a reminder here that good-quality fabric does not necessarily guarantee ease of manipulation when sewing. 'Good worsted is very difficult to work in small pieces because it is so springy, and silk mixtures are worse ...' Mary adds that although the tonal values were more limited than expected she found that the subtle differences could be positive qualities. No delaying tactic was employed here for claiming the need for more fabric!

Careful measurement with the aid of the weave and the use of a dual-feed foot on the machine were essential for the required precision.

Mary has never made traditional quilts but has been influenced and inspired by them. As a member of the Quilt Art group, whose philosophy commits members to serious and exploratory quilt-making, she wants to see a great variety and expects 'craftsmanlike consolidation and links with work of other media'.

Although this professional quilter is not employed, she does work five to ten hours a day when immersed in a project. She sells her work occasionally at exhibitions but more often on commission. As with many quilters, the top of the house is her 'studio'.

Her designs are composed of many coloured strips sewn together horizontally or vertically. If this seems like an easy way to make a quilt, when you see her many variations of theme, texture and technique you realise that it is Mary's own particular 'magic' that makes each hanging a pieced work of three-dimensional art: a desert, a roll of fabric, or the encapsulation of the smartness of the City.... These and many more suggest that there has been training in her background as a painter.

Mary's work can be seen in many books and has been included in television programmes, besides having been selected for exhibitions from 1982 onwards in many countries. It has also appeared in several Quilt Art collections and others in Britain.

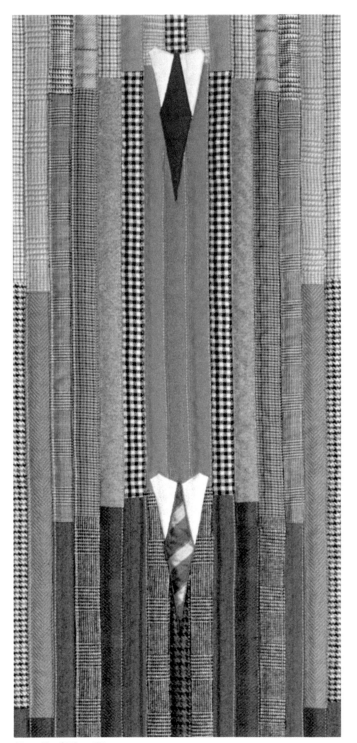

Detail of The City.

20

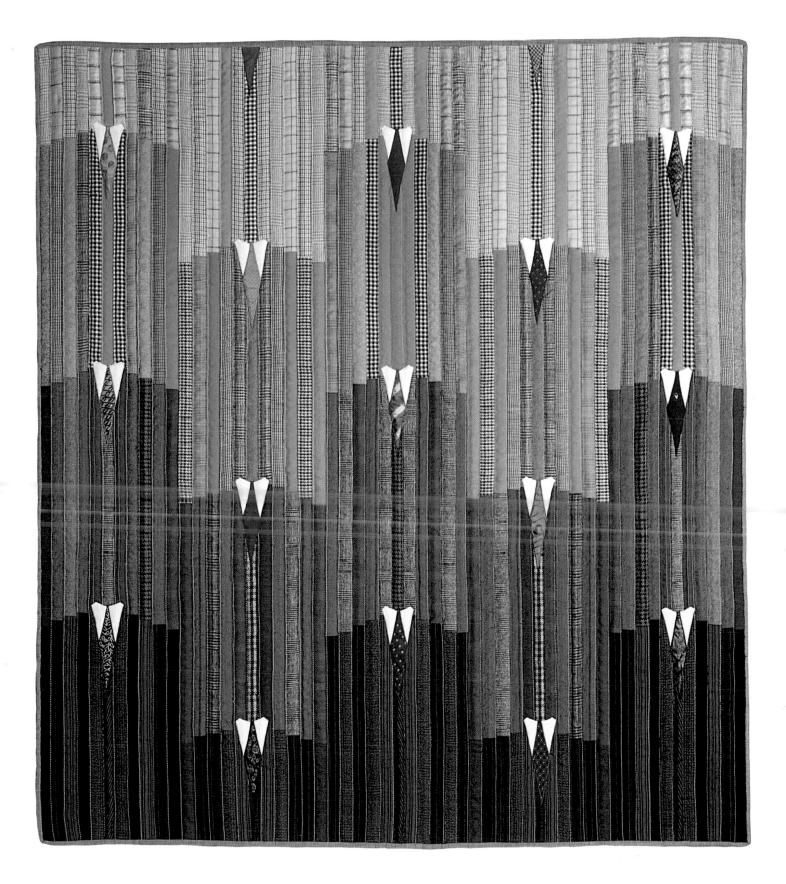

Original size: 120 x 132cm (48 x 53in).

Blowing in the Wind
and Farbenspiel (Play of Colours)

IRENA GOOS

Gansingen, Switzerland

B*lowing in the Wind* was designed spontaneously by Irena as she moved her pencil over a large sheet of paper. She says, 'I thought about my problems [and was] looking for solutions.' An interesting composition of lines emerged. She gave them a frame and added bright colours that depended on her mood at the time. Irena says that the problems had taken shape but the solutions were still 'blowing in the wind'.

First Irena made templates of the design. To obtain this kind of precision, she emphasises the need for practice and patience – and the use of a good sewing

Original size: both 97 x 110cm (39 x 44in).

22

machine with a dual feed, so that the layers of the quilt do not slip apart under the presser foot.

There are fifty points at the end of the 'leaves' of this wall-hanging: a superb example of curved piecing, with quilting in the ditch. There is strong movement in this small quilt, as indeed there is in the next one.

Farbenspiel (Play of Colours) produces the powerful visual illusion of two spirals appearing to open like springs as pieced bands of the colour spectrum curl round each other. This intricacy demands that the watcher take time to study its evolvement.

Irena says that she is 'fascinated by space, light and movement'. This is one of her series of quilts based on free geometric design.

Most of her quilts are designed on a visual display unit and reveal a sophisticated use of this aid. It is not simply that a single pattern is being repeated by the computer. Rather, here a unit is being varied in colour and developed spatially in relation to similar units to produce a sense of movement. The narrow but essential spaces in the coils maximise the three-dimensional

hollowness as the colours of the 'inside' are revealed.

Irena began quilting in 1984 with traditional patterns but soon started to develop her own designs. She has a room for storing fabric equipment and finished work and another for designing and sewing by machine. In addition to being exhibited in Switzerland, Irena's work has been selected for collections in thirteen international shows in the U.S.A., Germany, France and England.

Irena has never attended a course on patchwork or quilting, yet her work is admired and readily recognised throughout the contemporary quilting world. It seems, as for most of us, that creative need must find constant expression.

Carl Rogers, in *Towards a Theory of Creativity*, states: 'The mainspring of creativity appears to be the same tendency which we discover so deeply as the curative force in psychotherapy – man's tendency to actualise himself, to become his potentialities.' As quilters we are fortunate indeed to have been placed in an environment that fosters our creativity.

Farbenspiel
(right).

Blowing in
the Wind
(left).

Crazy Stars

KATHARINE GUERRIER
Worcester, England

Crazy Stars is one of a series using a block of crazy shapes. Its design was influenced by one of the Log Cabin arrangements, *i.e.* a block divided diagonally into light and dark halves. Four dark and four light triangles were then put together to form squares. Simple? Yes, but look at the way the colour and piecing were carefully planned at the corners of each square so that the four points of the star contrasted with the background.

The result is a lovely timeless design, easy to live with. Yet herein lies an unusual combination of fabrics: we look and look again, discovering scraps of batik, marbled fabric and other arresting prints. There is a strong turquoise with a strident black stripe in there somewhere, but it is hidden like an exotic bird in the sunlight and shadow of a rain forest.

Katharine has made traditional quilts: she modifies them to give a contemporary feel. At present she is interested in the decorative arts and will continue to work towards textiles that are 'desirable, collectable and original.' She is well along that road.

Her work is well known throughout the U.K. She also gives slide lectures and is a popular teacher, a 'giver' who enables her students to improve their technical skills and, thus reassured, to learn to release their own creativity.

Although Katharine attended art college in the 1960s, it was only after a visit to the U.S.A. that she turned to quilting. Her work has been selected for exhibitions in the U.K., the U.S.A. and Denmark, and for some years she has organised an exhibition at the Forge Mill Needle Museum, Redditch, in the summer months.

Original size: 145 x 145cm (58 x 58in).

24

Eothen

BARBARA HALLAS
Leeds, England

Eothen, or Traces of Travel Brought Home from the East, is the title of a book by Alexander Kinglake which was published in 1844. It was said of it at the time that it evoked 'the East itself in vital and actual reality'.

The main inspiration for the quilt was Paul Klee's painting *Tunisia*. Looking at the painting and at the quilt it is obvious that the domes of the mosques are the main common factor; many differences developed during the making of the quilt. First, five long strips of cotton cloth were coloured with fabric paint in a fairly patchy method. These strips were put on the lawn to dry and to fix the paint. It looked too much like a copy and so was bundled into a cupboard.

Two years later, after I had hunted for all the pieces, I painted out large sections of it and painted in other features. Now it really was ready for the waste bin!

Abandoned again to the depths of the attic, it was unearthed six months later. I chopped it into rectangles and spread it out on the sitting-room floor for everyone to walk past. The comments varied from a laughing 'What is it?' to 'Finish it and we'll see how it looks.' With such enthusiasm I could not help but complete it. It just had to be finished. I painted it again, appliquéd balconies, a palm tree, a flight of steps, and anything I imagined was Tunisian. Luckily, I started to like it.

At this point I decided to use free machine embroidery as a method of quilting and varied the pattern in every section. I seemed to be gliding over the surface for days. When it was finished I hoped that it had become truly mine, as it now appeared a brighter, more cheerful place than that Klee had painted.

Detail of Eothen.

Original size: 127 x 127cm (51 x 51in).

Untitled

BRIDGET INGRAM-BARTHOLOMÄUS
Berlin, Germany

Bridget's lovely quilt is luxury indeed, for not only is it almost all silk, a 'slippery customer' to handle, but also all the small pieces are hand-sewn over papers with absolute precision. The effect is of a multicoloured open-weave cloth.

There are five nesting squares. The outer one, or border, is densely machine-quilted with two small areas left unquilted which nicely provoke more interest. Inside the blue border there are about 600 units making up the first 'woven' square. This surrounds another square which is a variation in that the weave is on the diagonal and the strips have become narrower. Moving inwards the weave is again

horizontal and finer. The middle square is relatively tiny and the delicate weave is again on the diagonal.

There is a logical sequence to the pattern from the centre out which viewers find satisfying, a tried and tested arrangement similar to that of a medallion quilt. Yet this quilt is too intricate to fit into that category: it does not make abrupt changes of shape and size. The colours are carefully placed so that the deeper moss greens and the bright turquoise are not immediately apparent, but rather 'release' their contrast slowly.

What magic there was here to turn a bag of scraps into an exquisite silken quilt!

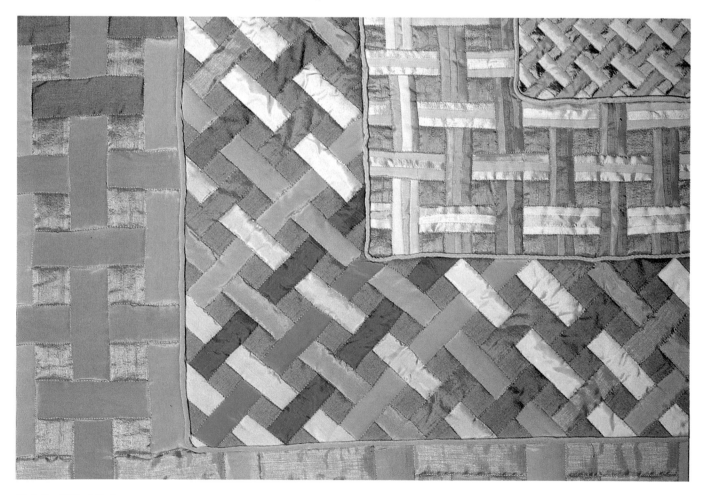

Detail of Untitled.

28

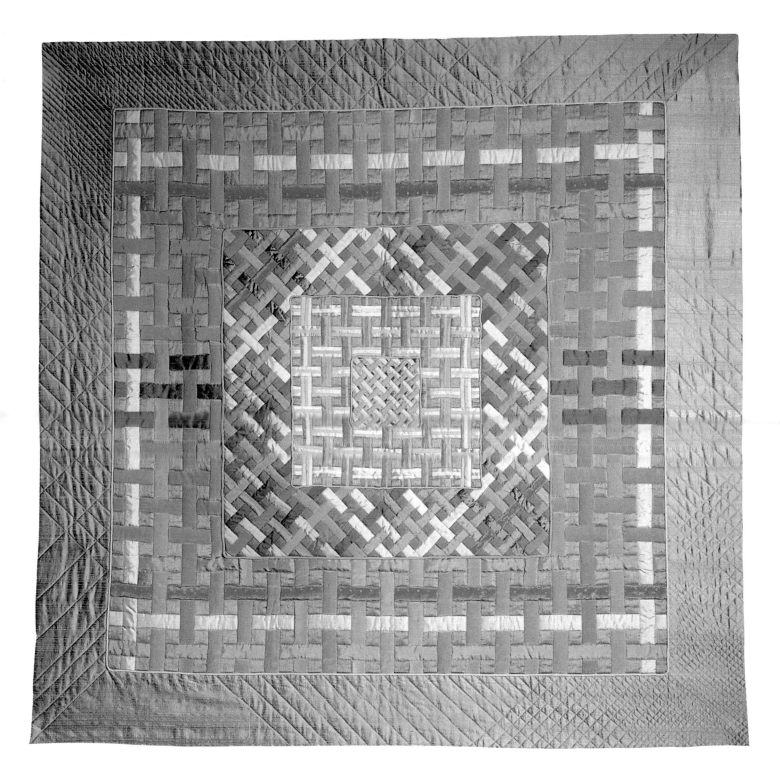

Original size: 170 x 170cm (68 x 68in).

Coming Out of the Wood

BRIDGET INGRAM-BARTHOLOMÄUS
Berlin, Germany

*C*oming Out of the Wood was made a few years after Bridget's *Untitled* piece, yet it is a development from that. The fifty or so chevron strips are made of many pieces so that a perfect match has again to be accomplished. There are hundreds of points and any one out of line would be immediately apparent. It shows considerable skill at the planning stage and with the machining. A dual feed, or equivalent, on the foot would be essential to prevent the three layers from slipping apart.

Bridget does have a rotary cutter but she still likes to use scissors.

The colours could be those of early leaves and their tiny shadows in the spring, while the pinks match the blossom of a magnificent hawthorn outside my window. You can almost feel those trailers brush against your face as you walk under the trees. The lower edge has a casual unevenness which somehow 'works'. All in all, this is a lovely, evocative piece.

Original size: 117 x 117cm (47 x 47in).

Opium Trail

LYN LAMBERT
Hampshire, England

O*pium Trail*, which is a very big quilt, was created as a problem-solving exercise for the City and Guilds Creative Studies Certificate Part 1. Here Lyn kindly takes us through her assignment step by step.

The inspiration was Monet's *Poppyfields at Giverny.* She chose to illustrate the life of the poppy. From seedhead to the bud stage, to the opening flower and then the full bloom (these measuring 23cm (9in) across), the whole cycle is laid before us. The design is thus very different from that of the usual flower quilt.

Several sets of templates with registration marks were needed for each poppy stage and these, together with the appropriate fabric pieces, were marshalled into marked plastic bags.

Moving outwards through concentric circles there are eight seed-heads, surrounded by a continuous 'stem' of buds, beyond which is a stylised band of more buds within small triangles. The flowers open out in the next area before, finally, the huge poppies themselves with their fragile petals abandon restriction and 'grow' towards the borders. The whole quilt is aglow with colour: a magnificent flowerbed and a superb piece of work.

The necessary steps which could not be skipped included hand piecing of the large poppies; putting them all on Vilene to keep the colour true; and hand application to the background. There were twenty large ones, and then there were the small ones to do as well....

Lyn used the machine for the straight lines of the border.

Finally, there was the quilting by hand and the embellishment, using cottons, polycottons and glazed cotton in seventy-nine different shades, and twenty-two shades of thread as well as quilting thread. In all, she logged up 900 hours. It is not surprising that Lyn has learnt a tremendous amount. If you have a 'spare' year ahead, this sort of quilt would be a marvellous thing to do.

Detail of Opium Trail.

Original size: 205 x 265cm (82 x 106in).

33

Ocean Blue

JANE LLOYD
County Antrim, Northern Ireland

I f blue is your favourite colour, then this quilt is the one for you! However, there are many colours here, which bring the quilt 'alive'. To collect a similar range, choose a colour and then add others, stronger and weaker, but still close together on the spectrum. This is a successful way of enlivening what might have been a relatively large flat blue area which would quickly have become boring to the eye. Jane has achieved much variation and as a result viewers' interest is kept alive as they scan this wall-hanging. It holds our attention even though there is not a figure or a definite recognisable pattern to be seen. All in all, it is a pleasing, well-planned quilt.

If you are wanting to make a contemporary wall-hanging, this would be a good place to start: use scraps, sew short seams by hand or machine, and enjoy playing about with colour. Jane has generously given us a few clues about the construction. Additional suggestions are included for piecing.

Method

Use a fine but firm backing fabric or fine Vilene. Cut a few scraps in a selection of your chosen colours. The scraps will look clumsy if the area of each is bigger than 5 x 5cm (2 x 2in) square. Make the shapes irregular. As a general rule, cut as small a piece as you can easily handle, including a 6mm ($^1/_4$in) seam allowance on all sides.

Place a scrap on the background and secure with a pin. Take a second scrap and with right sides together sew along one edge, securing these two scraps to each other and to the background. Open out the scrap and sew a third one to it, then continue until the area is covered.

With this method there will be three thicknesses of top fabric together with the backing fabric on each short seam. This needs to be taken into account if hand quilting is to follow. If, in addition, wadding is required between the backing and the top, the thickness increases.

Jane solved the problem by crazy-piecing on to a blanket and then quilting the completed top by machine, with the option of using an invisible nylon filament in the needle and the usual thread on the bobbin. The blanket proved to be a firm foundation, enabling the quilt to hang straight.

The filler depends on the fineness or otherwise of the fabrics used and the required finished weight of the work. Also, crazy patchwork can be done without a middle layer of wadding. After adding her strip border, Jane sewed on the lining in the same way as you would on a curtain, *i.e.* right sides together and all four edges sewn around, leaving an opening.

Turn the quilt the right side out and slip-stitch the opening edges together.

Colour organisation

Dyeing some of the fabric helped coordinate the colours. You can use your washing machine for dyeing: it is quick, easy and permanent. Putting mixed cotton prints into the same dye produces many surprises and a useful 'family' of tints and shades – the only drawback is that using several dyes can work out expensive if only small amounts of fabric are being dyed.

In Jane's quilt only some of the fabrics are dyed. This blue quilt consists of scraps of lavenders, purples, greens, and turquoise.

The thing to do is to divide your area into workable dimensions of perhaps four blocks of 50 x 40cm (20 x 16in) and decide where the lightest and darkest colours should be in this rectangle. Arrange piles of neatly trimmed scraps into light, medium and dark tones, then crazy-piece together mixtures of these on to the backing.

It is usually more satisfying to create than to copy, so try a new idea, for example cliffs and sand, trees and undergrowth, or sunrise and waves, all subjects that lend themselves to crazy patchwork.

Original size: 127 x 95cm (51 x 38in).

Not a Granny's Flower Garden

IRENE MACWILLIAM

Belfast, Northern Ireland

In quilting there are various styles of grouping, one of which is 'Grandmother's Flower Garden', where a multitude of coloured fabric scraps can be utilised. Although occasionally a beautiful hexagon quilt will be seen at an exhibition, for many of us it is the need for variety that beguiles us into going 'beyond the garden gate'. Irene has gone far beyond, into the realms of distinction.

This quilt is newer than her appliquéd events-of-the-year quilts and other evocative machine-embroidered and appliquéd pieces. Irene says that she was surprised to find herself making a quilt with flowers! Many fabrics were incorporated, especially shiny ones such as silk, taffeta and polyester. The difficulty of handling these was overcome by machining them on to a Vilene base before doing the hand quilting.

The design in this quilt is a variation of 'Log Cabin', which consists of fabric strips surrounding a centre square, representing the fire in the pioneer cabins of the U.S.A. and Canada. Strips on two adjacent sides represent the light, and those on the other sides the shadow.

As for its origins, an American book mentions its use for the mummy wrappings of antiquity and dates its later appearance in England as being in the early 1800s. However, apparently the American quiltmaker developed it, varied it and made it a quilt classic.

The Log Cabin pattern is suitable for the beginner. It is found in many quilt books and should perhaps be attempted before the 'Pineapple' variation.

Irene has accomplished this variation by limiting the spectrum of colours for the 'flowers'. In this pattern the logs 'move' out from the centre square and diminish towards the corners of the block, while the logs have become narrow trapezoids with jagged edges. Colour selection here needs care in order to achieve the desired effect. One of these effects is the visual illusion of rotation which can give a feeling of excitement to the work.

Irene does not feel compelled to purchase a lot of fabric before starting a quilt; rather, she prefers to take what she already has and spread it out on the floor. Then she sorts and re-sorts it into piles of suitable colours. She never has a pre-conceived idea of how big

the quilt will be: '...things evolve. I used the Pineapple block to get the idea of coloured flowers weaving across the surface.' Coloured spots, already embroidered on the silk when purchased, appear at random intervals, giving added interest to the finished hanging. This exquisite quilt illustrates again the possibilities of Log Cabin and its derivatives: changes of 'mood' available through colour choice and the juxtaposition of the values of the positive and negative elements of the pattern.

The pattern 'Court-House Steps' has the 'logs' placed symmetrically about a central axis. All these arrangements, together with the 'settings' of the light and shade of each block, enable a patchworker to produce beautiful and original work for decades. Start here if you wish to make a quilt relatively quickly, are able to sew a straight line for about twelve inches on a sewing machine, and do not particularly want to hand-quilt. Here is ample opportunity to play about with colours and scraps of fabric.

Keep your logs 2cm (^{3}/$_4$in) wide plus a 6mm (^{1}/$_4$in) seam allowance along each side, thus avoiding the wide logs of the quilt-in-a-day variety. Find a deserted corner of the house which you do not have to tidy daily and just keep sewing.

Detail of Not a Granny's Flower Garden.

Original size: 130 x 190cm (52 x 76in).

Migration Indienne (Indian Migration)

SUZON DE MARCILLY

Plessey-Robinson, France

The inspiration for this quilt came from one made in Tennessee in 1871 by Elizabeth Baxter as a wedding present to her son Robert and his wife Sarah Jane. It has now been given by the family to Newport-Cocke County Museum in the U.S.A.

Suzon's pointed tepees appear identical to those of the original. However, there the likeness seems to end, as she has designed her quilt so that the small pieced patterns radiate or migrate from the centre. A present-day quilt-maker would of course be likely to have a much greater choice of colours and fabric than Mrs Baxter had.

For the background Suzon has chosen a warm yellow that suggests the dried earth of a hot North American summer. Elizabeth Baxter's quilt pattern is probably original. It would be interesting to know how she came to plan it and what she would have thought of Suzon's variation 122 years later! In New College, Oxford, it hung at the far end of the room so that visitors were attracted to it from a distance. The tepees are composed of such tiny pieces that they appear at first glance to be printed; on closer inspection one is amazed to see that every little triangle is pieced.

There is no less than a quarter of a kilometre, or one-sixth of a mile, of hand quilting, and that, amongst textile artists, must be a marathon. In every sense of the word this is a very fine example of piecing and quilting. It is to be hoped that one day Suzon will see the quilt which originally inspired her.

Detail of Migration Indienne.

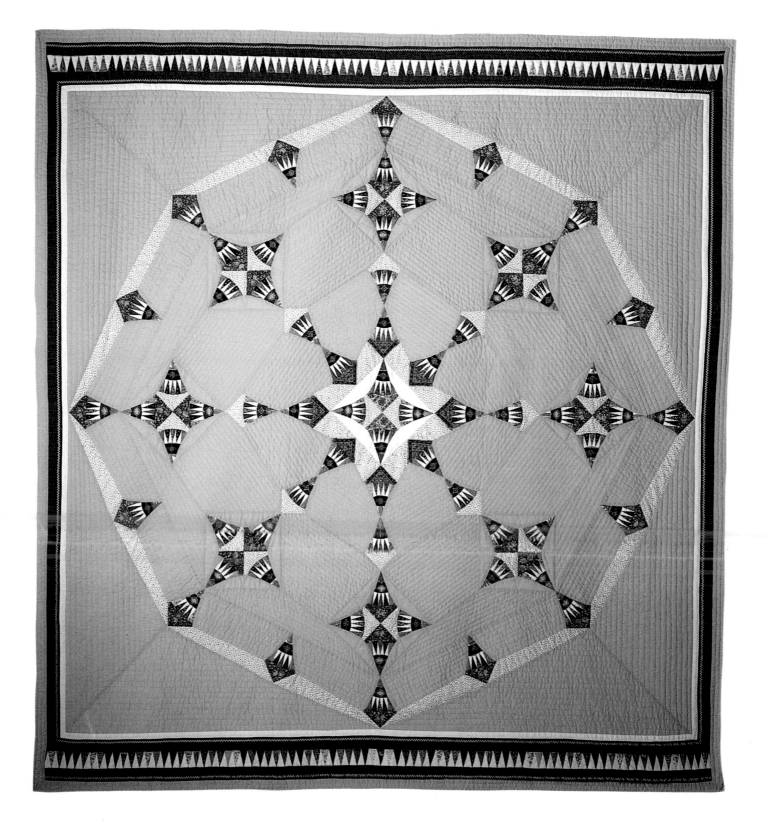

Original size: 187 x 202cm (75 x 81in).

The Lilac Fountain

MARIA-LUISE MEYER
Witten-Bommern, Germany

This is a large quilt, yet it is beautifully light and soft to handle. Each individual spray of water has a light-coloured upper edge and a darker lower one. The movement of the fountain is convincingly achieved by the use of curved piecing and by the finely graded colours. One can almost see the water shooting up from the dark base and through the sun's rays before falling outwards.

The arcs vary in density of colour from purplish brown to lightest lilac and almost white as the 'water' rises. The 'bricks' of the background are in many tints and tones of grey.

An inner border is hand quilted in a Weardale pattern from the north of England, 'Old Joe's Chain'. Surrounding this is another border of diagonal strips utilising all the colours of the fountain.

This quilt is lively, disciplined and delightful, and after I had seen it every day for several weeks, it still looked fresh and pleasing. It does not pose a problem or offer a surprise, but it slowly 'rewards' repeated viewing by revealing its subtlety of design and skill.

Marlis, a retired medical consultant, started quilting in 1985 and is mainly self-taught, though she is a member of a very active group in Dortmund. For her, quilting had become more than a part-time hobby; she wanted to be involved in it, as she says , '... as long as I live'. I think that all the quilters mentioned in this book have the same desire!

Making quilts, and gardening in summer, take up much of Marlis's time; she travels abroad each year and seeks out quilts whenever possible. Her work has been exhibited in Britain, Switzerland, France, Germany and the U.S.A. She strongly recommends having a room of one's own; although of course many of us have to wait for such a room until our children leave home!

It is reassuring to be a member of a quilt group meeting monthly or more often, but generally we are more likely to create truly original work when we work alone.

Detail of The Lilac Fountain.

Original size: 180 x 200cm (72 x 80in).

Alaskan Glacier

REE NANCARROW AND KARLA HARRIS
Alaska, U.S.A.

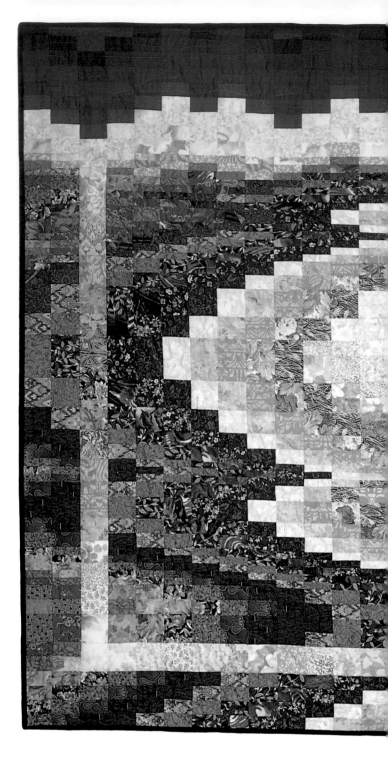

T his quilt is the view from its owners' lodge, which is located in full view of Mount McKinley in Denali National Park, U.S.A. The commission was given to Ree and her sister Karla, who then discussed the subject-matter, size and general feel of what was wanted with their clients. Techniques and colours were selected as work proceeded, and there was constant evaluation of how subsequent strips of colour would project when placed next to those already in place.

The patchwork equivalent of Bargello tonal gradations, so named after the embroidery pieces displayed in the Bargello Palace, Florence, was a happy choice for *Alaskan Glacier*, with its deep perspective. There are about twenty different greens and blues in the left-hand section and many more colours on the calm glacier itself. The two textile artists make us aware of

Detail of Alaskan Glacier.

Original size: 210 x 125cm (84 x 50in).

the weight of the glacier as it flows down from the ice-capped mountains, ever widening, and even defying the inner border as it continues its age-old insidious progress; beautiful, awesome and relentless.

Many quilts have an inner border, but it is frequently used to bring the design to a halt, or to let a small section stray outwards. Here its function is much more subtle: there is perhaps a hint of control, but this is wisely omitted from the deep blue of the 'sheltering sky', which has its own kind of presence.

There is joyful relief, for the flowers of the Alaskan spring are pieced in a surprisingly bright pink and other carefully chosen fabrics, reassuring us of nature's renewed activity.

Karla lives in Idaho and Ree in Alaska. Both have workrooms and are organised about their work, and they managed to plan this quilt together successfully.

Karla has been quilting for eight years and has taught classes. She enjoys having several quilt projects developing at the same time. She finds that work on one will often prove to be a solution on another.

Ree has been a self-employed artist for over twenty-five years, working with textiles and also using silk-screen painting, weaving and needlepoint. She averages forty-eight hours a week: '...I work incessantly on a piece once it is begun, doing whatever it takes to solve it.' When the sisters work together, they stop only to eat and have six hours' sleep.

Both sisters have had their quilts selected for books and both have won prizes in the U.S.A. They are fortunate in having a mother who was skilled with a needle and a grandmother who made a living as a dressmaker when patterns were not available. Ree states that as well as learning from books she has acquired skills from her sister.

Karla's younger daughter Wynona has had a custom-quilting business for three years and quilted *Alaskan Glacier*. Like many accomplished textile artists, the sisters find it hard to decide to let their quilts go, but we hope nevertheless that we will have the privilege of seeing their future work.

Make Hay While the Sun Shines

JACKIE NEVILL
Dorset, England

This is another large quilt. It was made for the final assessment of the City and Guilds certificate in Patchwork and Quilting Part 1.

A print of a painting was the source for the designs and Jackie ended up with Monet's *Haystacks: End of Summer*, although it was not her choice, and she said that she would not have chosen it had she known what was in store over the next two years!

First Jackie investigated the effects of colours on each other; then, having thought of the title, she proceeded to design a quilt to fit. The colours are those of the sun on the landscape at different times of the day. The sun beams down from the top left of the quilt so fiercely that the colour is, realistically, almost bleached from the scene. When this shaft of bright sunlight becomes more diffuse, the haystacks appear warmer. As the strongest shadow is next to the brightest light, the adjacent diagonals of haystacks beyond the rays are surrounded by darker hues.

This gradation of colour, the very essence of Jackie's design concept, is wrought painstakingly by the piecing of an infinite number of small strips of fabric to form the 126 haystacks and intervening spaces. The hand quilting also plays a relevant role as the group of upward-curving lines reminds us of tossing the hay.

Monet may not have painted with such precision as Jackie has, but here Jackie has created the impression brilliantly.

Detail of Make Hay While the Sun Shines.

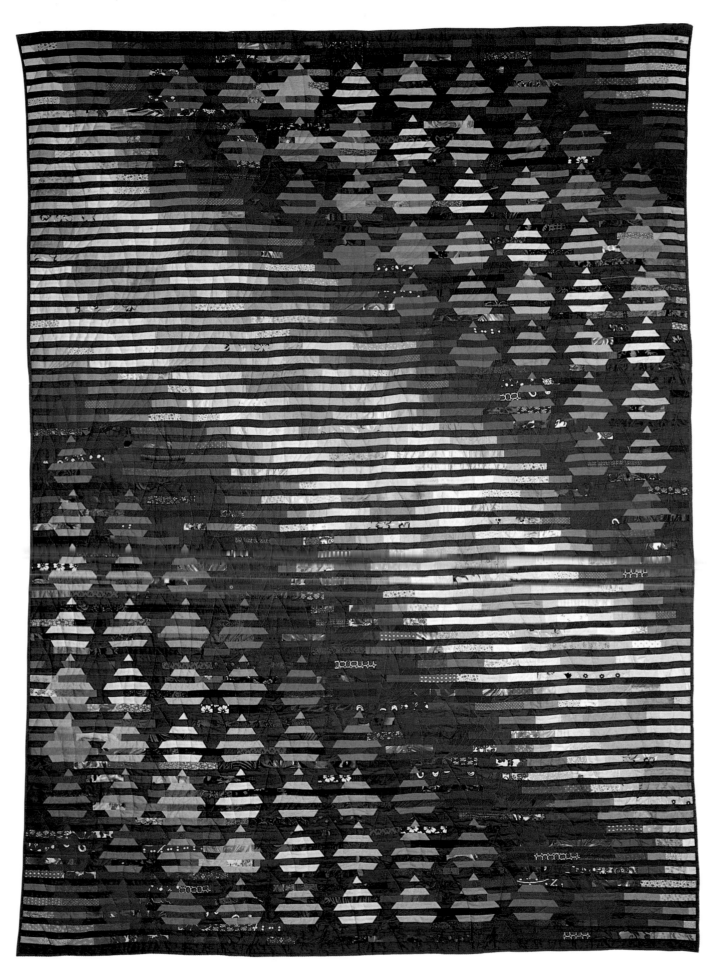

Original size: 177 x 240cm (71 x 96in).

Future History

AUDREY NICHOLS
Maine, U.S.A.

(Kindly loaned by the owner, Mrs Judy Redding, who commissioned it)

This is a strange and fascinating wall-hanging. Audrey says, 'The title refers to those aspects of history not commonly expressed in history books... A better understanding of our past could change the way we perceive the world and our place in it.' In her quilt she has painted images that are representations of authentic paintings and carvings.

The painted cave of Altamira in Northern Spain was decorated by Stone-Age man. In 1879 a Spanish landowner went into the cave to excavate for artefacts, accompanied by his nine-year-old daughter, who happened to look up and discover the painted ceiling. Here was the bison that Audrey has stencilled on to her work.

On the right is a copy of a 'Venus' figure, and below is a painting of one of the small 'Chinese' horses found on a wall in the famous Lascaux cave in south-west France, discovered in September 1940 by four boys. It has the best-preserved paintings yet found. As man had this artistic ability even 35,000 years ago, it is not surprising that a modern-day artist is interested and excited and feels that she wants to relate in some way.

Audrey presents several other copies of cave drawings, along with embellishments representing various cultures.

At the top of the quilt there is a sky section in the form of a helix made up of twenty-six different blue fabrics. High in this area are several covered buttons painted with care to represent the phases of the moon, from crescent and gibbous to full.

Audrey has made clever use of her fabrics: a yard-long snake stretches itself across the width of the hanging as fifteen printed figures dance beneath. At the base a goddess rises up amid Fortuny fabric flames. Beads, shells, and representations of artefacts adorn the pieced border at intervals.

This is certainly a most original and intriguing wall-hanging. Audrey's skills, together with the rich vein of prehistory she has mined, could start her off on creating a whole series!

Detail of Future History.

Original size: 95 x 162cm (38 x 65in).

46

Mother Earth's Birthwaters

AUDREY NICHOLS
Maine, U.S.A.

This quilt gives you the impression of being right in the middle of the winter woods with the sun just rising and warming the scene a little, while the rushing water and the melting snow suggest that the brook will soon be in full spate.

The quilting appears mainly in the water, with the froth depicted by a raw-edged lace-like fabric. There is a restrained use of Japanese prints of water, and four blues increase in value as they flow downwards. The perspective is convincing, aided by the tree trunks' and the rocks' increasing in size towards the front of the scene. Five subtle shades of velvet moss and lichen grow on the rocks alongside fine tweeds, providing texture as well as light and shade.

Audrey says of this quilt that the spring floods are the start of the season of rebirth. 'The life/death/ rebirth cycle of life is suggested in the hand-quilted and beaded border. The plants release their seeds in the wind.' Their growth creates a never-ending cycle. A vet who saw the quilt remarked that in his experience the water was a little pinker! Audrey was interested, perhaps, in the not-so-smooth cycle.

The blocks of the pieced border each contain as many as twelve coloured fabrics, and no two blocks have the same colour combination. The increasing force of life in the supporting brook becomes more dominant as the water from the tributary crashes into the pool and 'flows' off the quilt into the widening world. All this was achieved with a variety of fabrics and techniques including painting, airbrushing, machine-piecing and appliqué.

Detail from Mother Earth's Birthwaters.

Original size: 165 x 180cm (66 x 72in).

Einsamkeit (Loneliness)

LIESEL NIESNER
Osnabrück, Germany

Liesel has been making quilts for about fifteen years and has made over ninety full-sized ones, a third of them being traditional ones. This particular one, *Einsamkeit*, was inspired by a holiday she spent in a secluded village in Switzerland. She says, 'Because of the environmental problems present even in this little community, I had a vision of a totally empty landscape without any living creature.'

Liesel won the Quilt Art category, using the same theme on a different quilt, at the Great British Quilt Festival, Nostell Priory, Yorkshire, in 1988. In *Einsamkeit* she did not want the outline of the blocks to be obvious, so she had to ensure careful matching of the bands of colour flowing into and out of each block. Many trials and adjustments had to be made, as it was necessary to plan not only a single block but also the eight surrounding ones, just as repeating patterns are planned for printed fabrics. There are two spiders' webs hidden in the quilting, and within the dark border the quilting pattern echoes the outline of the bands in a satisfactory way.

The result is original and was a winner in the 1988 American Quilters' Society Exhibition, Paducah, for the most innovative use of the medium, and was the overall winner in the Contemporary International Quilt Collection at New College, Oxford, and Nostell Priory, Yorkshire, in 1993.

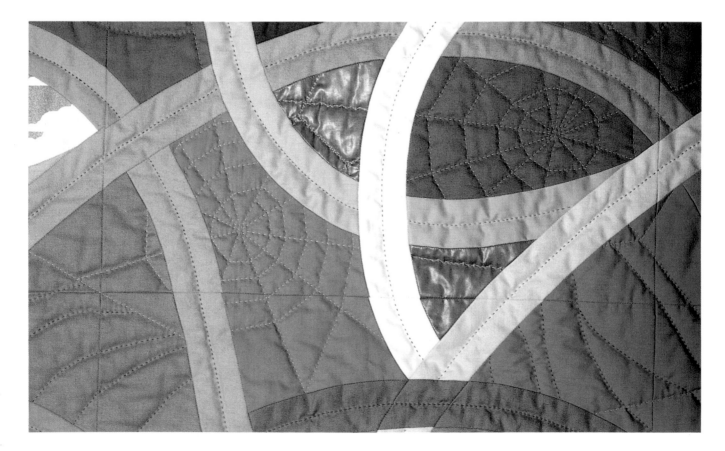

Detail from Einsamkeit.

Original size: 145 x 210cm (58 x 84in).

Liesel's work has also been selected for exhibitions in other areas of the U.S.A. and Canada, and also in Switzerland and Germany.

Although Liesel Niesner's name is well known in the quilting world, it is rather comforting to know that she still uses what might be called the old-fashioned methods: home-made cardboard templates, the use of scissors (restricting the use of her rotary cutter to strips), and using two pins plus notching the concave seam to ensure a flat curve. However, judging by present performance, her designs are likely to be in the leading group as we move into the twenty-first century.

'Ich Fand Meine Blaue Blume' (I have found my Blue Flower)

LIESEL NIESNER
Osnabrück, Germany

Many visitors to the exhibition thought that of the two quilts of Liesel's which were displayed, this one should have been the winner. Both are quite lovely. There is much variation in the quilting patterns in this piece, including another spider's web.

The title, 'I have found my "blue flower"', refers to the motif of 'longing and searching for the unattainable' in the novel *Heinrich von Ofterdingen*, by the German writer Novalis. Heinrich never did find his 'blaue Blume', but happily Liesel has!

Liesel's daughter was the first in the home to make a quilt, when she was fifteen. She put squares of fabric together 'to make a pattern like a crossword'. All the family admired it and then Liesel made one herself, although in Germany at that time she had never heard of patchwork and quilting. A year later her daughter's exchange student brought her a quilt book from England, and Liesel was 'hooked'. She loves working with fabric and colour and prefers to use pure cottons. She has sold a few quilts but sometimes finds it hard to let them go!

Often she hears someone declare that it is absolutely impossible to quilt (well) without a frame or hoop. They must go mute when they look at Liesel's quilting. Those of us who are hopeless sigh with relief.

Detail of 'Ich Fand Meine Blaue Blume'.

Original size: 155 x 190cm (62 x 76in).

Nautilus

GISELA PUGNI-SPATZ

Freiburg, Germany

Here we have a tropical mollusc: a spiral chambered cell, a sort of diving-bell. A blue sea is predictable, but having the shells in similar colours seems inspired and is more restful than a contrast would have been.

An odd number of differently sized spirals offers interest as the eye is taken round the quilt. There are between seventeen and twenty-one segments in many tones and shades of the blues, in both shiny and matt fabrics. Each wedge shape is padded trapunto-fashion so that there is depth to the quilting, and flatter quilting represents the movement of the water. As the colours descend, the value increases, giving a sense of depth to the sea.

As with other work of Gisela's, tiny triangles of a gold-coloured fabric are scattered about, providing highlights that sparkle in the 'water'.

Gisela had previously made a quilt picturing snails. She spent some time planning the shape, as this demands mathematical precision if it is to look convincing. Next came *Nautilus*. Plans of the shapes were made on paper and used as templates, and then the whole thing was pieced by hand, taking care to achieve soft changes of colour.

Gisela made four traditional quilts and then lost interest for a few years. However, after seeing an exhibition in Germany in 1991, she became fascinated by contemporary work and is now creating her own designs. This wall-hanging portrays a peaceful underwater existence.

Detail from Nautilus.

Original size: 117 x 147cm (47 x 59in).

Fernblick (Distant View)

ELKE SCHILLING
Hamburg, Germany

Rugged rocks and flowing water are depicted in this distant scene; the dense quilting creates crevasses and ledges on the mountains with waves and movement in the water around them. Elke wanted an effect of depth, so she achieved this with machine-like precision by taking great care.

First she drew the full-size design on paper and then did a copy of every part. Each triangle is a different size and was numbered. Then she made another set of copies, with the addition of a seam allowance.

Next, she cut the fabric and pinned it to a display wall so that she could see the effects of the colour and move the pieces about until she felt the effect was right. There are stronger blues and browns at the base, or, as it appears, the front, of the scene. The colours become cooler as they move into the distance and, together with the slight diminution of the triangles, the depth of perspective Elke hoped for is convincingly achieved. The hand quilting continues into the border.

As the light in the exhibition room constantly changed throughout the spring day, this quilt also changed. The shadows cast by the dense stitching created the illusion that there, just outside the window, was 'ein Fernblick'. This lovely quilt would have the effect of visually increasing the size of the smallest room.

Elke has exhibited in Germany, Hungary, France, Austria, Denmark and England.

Original size: 140 x 140cm (56 x 56in).

The Wedding in Ramallah

JUDITH TRAGER
Colorado, U.S.A.

Judith's striking quilt is a contemporary, one-of-a-kind sort of quilt. It is made up of strong, vibrant colours which people in Europe often associate with the heat of the Middle East and Africa, where pale tints can look rather insipid. Judith started with a printed fabric that looks like Oriental carpets, and also wanted to show the blacks, blues, reds and sandstone colours prevalent in Israel.

Judith tells us that *The Wedding in Ramallah* was inspired by the traditional wedding dresses Palestinian women inherit from older female relatives, each bride wearing a dress which is indigenous to her village or area. The Palestinian cities of the West Bank, including Jerusalem, are very old and the streets, which are narrow with lots of steps, are impassable to cars. Their sunbleached sandstone walls capture the life within: the souks; the cafés and the brides in traditional dress.

This quilt is a modern-day 'crazy', with arrays of log-cabin pieces giving structure to this asymmetrical design. An irregular half of the border is in a vibrant turquoise which matches a few of the logs, thus fulfilling the 'rule' of a correspondence between picture and frame. Discreet amounts of a copper-coloured lamé add a touch of zippiness. 'I try to let the quilt tell me where it is going,' Judith says, echoing what many other quilters are beginning to experience.

Judith does seem to have had the ideal quilter's existence. Starting in about 1950 she was the official needle-threader at her mother's 'quilting bees'. Over the next forty years her work evolved through traditional and non-traditional designs; currently she is excited by three-dimensional work such as fabric-layering, manipulation and embellishment. She is a full-time textile artist and also gives classes in her large new studio and elsewhere as an invited artist.

A good teacher, she thinks, should have patience, an ability to listen and to see a student's work with an open mind, a willingness to share knowledge and sometimes even secrets, and a generous spirit.

She has exhibited in Japan, Britain, and the U.S.A., including at the Smithsonian Institution.

Judith tried to be an artist in other media but quilt-making chose her! She admits that occasionally she still feels a need to make a 'real quilt', and although the feeling passes, traditional elements do appear in her contemporary work.

Detail of The Wedding in Ramallah.

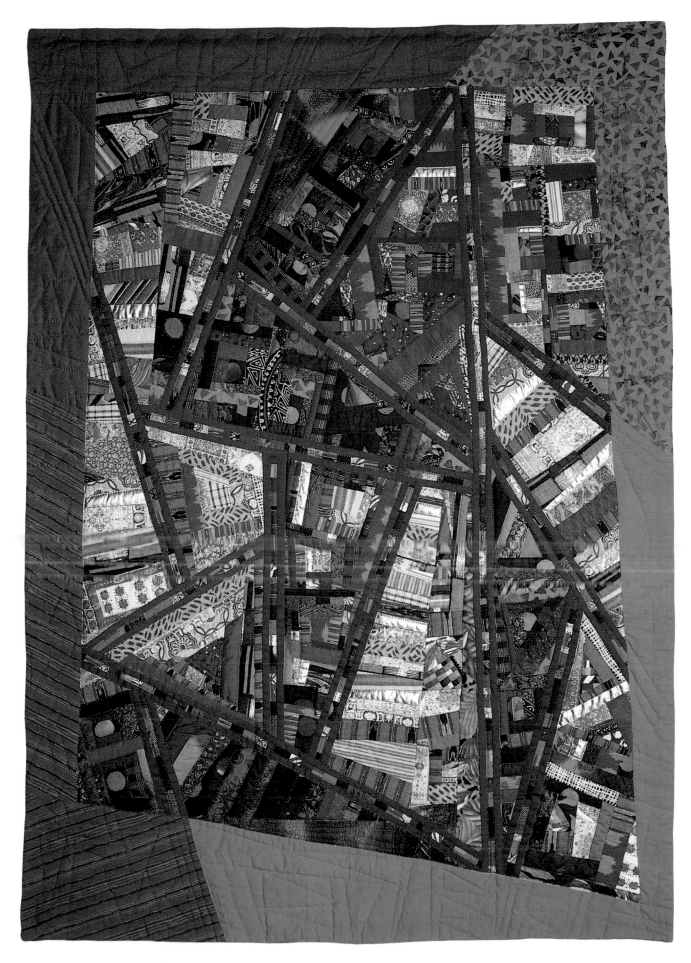

Original size: 115 x 162cm (46 x 65in).

Girls of Glory

ULVA UGERUP
Lund, Sweden

Ulva completed this stunning wall-hanging in 1992 and it is to hang permanently in the public library in Helsingborg, near Elsinore in Denmark.

The fabrics from her scrap-bag include cottons, wool, brocades, velvets, and viscose. The different textures, together with such colours as red, orange, pink and purple, interspaced with black, create a lush effect similar to that of an interior painted in the nineteenth century by Josefina Holmlund, a Swedish artist who mixed a richness of decoration within the rectangular spaces of rooms and doorways.

Here are ninety 'girls' who in Ulva's view have achieved something remarkable. The name of each is machine-embroidered in a small zigzag with bright yellow thread. This work is different from 'pretty' embroidery: it is a portrait gallery, dramatic, vibrant and fun. Where else would you find Colette, Mae West, Mary Kingsley, the Brontë sisters and P.D. James in a show together?

The hair on each head has some skilfully sewn personal variations: plaits for Elizabeth Garrett Anderson, bushy hair and a huge lace collar for Elizabeth Barrett Browning, and a neat style for Golda Meir. The light-coloured faces are 3.8cm (1½ in) ovals, drawn by machine and hand-appliquéd to each rectangle. Ulva made each face on the machine with a portrait of the girl in front of her, making no drawings or guidelines on the fabric.

Writing about quilting, Ulva says, 'It is a most humble and most sophisticated art, created by women to satisfy their longing for beauty.' This is not unlike the pioneer woman who with her scraps made her quilts as warm as she could so her family would not freeze and as beautiful as she could so her heart would not break.

Ulva delights us when she states, 'I love crazy', yet she would agree that nothing is as simple as it seems at first sight. For crazy patchwork to be successful it may need as much planning as any other type of quilt, and this was the case here.

Truly, this is an unusual and glorious wall-hanging.

Original size: 175 x 150cm (70 x 60in).
(Detail shown on page 3.)

Geometrische Vergnügung (Pleasure in geometry)

HELGA WEISE
Darmstadt, Germany

Helga says, 'Quilting is easy, but finding a name for the quilt is difficult.' Some artists would agree, but more of us do not realise that there is a problem and consequently our choice may not always be totally appropriate.

A description such as 'brown and fawn squares and triangles' may not sound like that of a winning quilt. The colour is restricted, but this actually contributes to the strength of the design: the limited use of brown checks, plain cream and burnt-sienna silks and similar fabrics produces a calm monochromatic surface. The simplicity of the shapes belies the design skill that created this piece.

The pattern for her quilt emerged as she played with a pair of compasses and a ruler. A physicist at Helga's place of work thought it was an illustration of Pythagoras' Theorem: 'the square on the hypotenuse equals the sum of the squares on the other two sides'.

Helga seems to have designed an original block for patchworkers consisting of eight long right-angled triangles and four smaller ones, all set in a square block and surrounding a central square. The fifteen blocks are hand quilted to follow the design. The quilting of the plain, relatively wide border is in generous 'free' curves, being a balanced contrast to the interior straight lines. The size of the quilt was determined by the piece of beige fabric given to Helga by a friend.

Helga has attended workshops given by American, English and German teachers, and she has exhibited in several local exhibitions.

Detail of Geometrische Vergnügung.

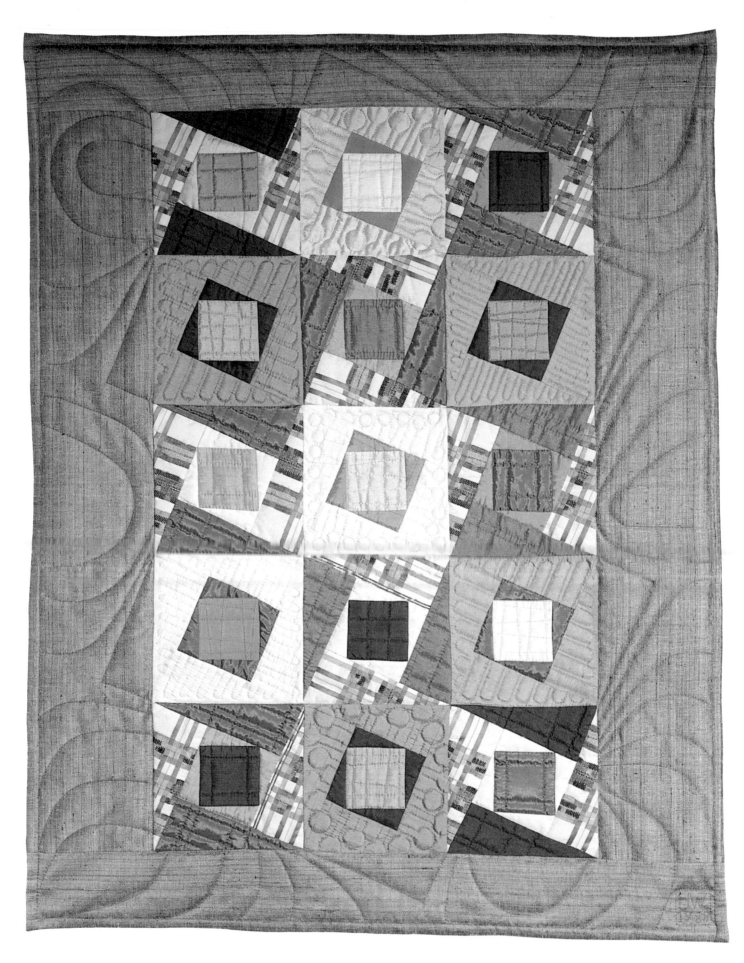

Original size: 90 x 115cm (36 x 46in).

INDEX